CULTURAL DEVASTATION IN THE NOVELS OF CHINUA ACHEBE

DR A HAZEL VERBINA

ISBN 979-888546765-0

Contents

Foreword *v*

1. Chapter 1 1

Foreword

This Book explores the devastation caused due to colonization in Chinua Achebe's Novels and it also brings about the transition in the cultural and traditional values of the Igbo tribe of Africa. The transition has been witnessed in different fragments and it is cxquisitely revealed in his trilogy and also in his other two novels. The author has identified the major elements and situations that led to the cultural exploitation and specifies the reason for the annihilation of the Igbo people.

CHAPTER ONE

"A civilization that uses its principles for trickery and deceit is a dying civilization Europe is indefensible" (Loomba, 154).

Africa had contacts with the other countries many years earlier to the original colonial expansion. The Europeans started their venture 500 years before, slowly towards the African continent. The European invasion brought profound changes among the culture, tradition and the individual, which brought drastic changes and consequences that led to the threat of the destruction of the native religion. "European commercial enterprise sought raw materials, cheap labour, new markets and even land culminating eventually in the colonial domination of almost the whole continent, a situation from which Africa has only emerged in relatively recent times" (Connor, 169) 'Africa' becomes split between a dying, traditional past which is at once hugely intrusive and obsolete, and banal modernity which is obsessed with interpreting an 'idea' of African identity. (Kanneh, 6)

Loomba identifies that the process of colonization was not an identical process in the parts of the world but the core component of colonization was undertaking or locking the originLoomba identifies that colonialism reshapes, often violently, physical territories, social terrains as well as human identities. As the Caribbean novelist George Lamming put it, 'The colonial experience is a live experience in the consciousness of these people. ... The experience is a continuing psychic experience that has to be dealt with and will have to be dealt with long after the actual colonial situation formally "ends"' (Hulme, 155).al inhabitants of the land. (7)

Taking into consideration the idea of Lommba this chapter discusses the idea of reshaping a country and its aftermaths. "Achebe has justly been called a chronicler, for in the last resort he is not dealing simply with the collapse of African society, but with its transformation. He is examining from the inside the historical evolution of African society at its moment of crisis, and the inevitable tensions attendant upon this process" (Whittaker, Msiska, 84)

Achebe's novels have been influential because of their acute capacity to map out the cultural fault in which African cultures and traditions have encountered the institutions of modern European colonial society (Gikandi, 10). Achebe's novels best 140 exemplify African traditional life and culture. Achebe's fascination towards the Ibo tribe and his urge to preserve its culture is depicted in his first novel *Things Fall Apart*. Achebe uses Igbo folk tales in his novels to demonstrate the traditions of his people. He employs them to evoke the workings of traditional Ibo society. *Things Fall Apart*, Achebe's first novel, as the title suggests, exposes the chaos in the Ibo society, which has a cultural past to boast of, like any other ancient civilization. "The battle over knowledge and the meaning of civilisation takes place most significantly over the issue of literacy, and the cognitive capacities which it demands and creates" (Kanneh, 27).

Cultural devastation is witnessed in various fragmentations. This chapter analyses these fragmentations on the basis of the colonizers' entry and its aftermaths affecting the culture step by step. The devastation caused is discussed on the basis of (i) an Identical crisis, (ii)Disintegration of structure, and (iii) the Distortion of customs, rituals, etc. According to Okot, a famous Uganda poet, the educational system imposed on the colonized people was the root cause of the cultural conflict. "The individual who goes through the school system eventually turns away from his cultural roots as he acquires more Western values" (Gikandi, 527).

Civilization is a changing pattern and the devastation it causes in society is the foremost idea of this chapter. This chapter deals with the different dimensions of the devastation. To begin with, *Things Fall Apart* is the hero's quest towards a perfect and traditional society. The colonizer's march is towards civilizing the Ibo tribe, for which they bring the religion Christianity. Okonkwo is not against the people's civilization but he thinks it is not necessary of him to covert himself to get civilized. The exploitation of Ibo culture, rituals, society and people is the major theme of Achebe's *Things Fall Apart*. Gohar Ayaz analyzes the Ibo community and how it is intruded on by the colonizers. The Ibo is the second largest group of people living in southern Nigeria. The Igbo has no common traditional story of their origin. Historians claim that the Ibo are descended from waves of immigrants from the north and the west who arrived in the fourteenth or fifteenth century in Nigeria. European contact with the Igbo began with the arrival of the Portuguese in the mid-fifteenth century in Nigeria. The Portuguese were the first Europeans to explore Nigeria. Though the Portuguese were the first people to enter Nigeria they were not able to conquer. So Achebe has not mentioned the Portuguese anywhere in the novel. The British entered Nigeria first through trade and then established The Royal Niger Colony in 1886 by shifting Nigeria's culture in order to their own. The success of the colony led to Nigeria becoming a British territory in 1901. Igbo is one of the major societies at that time that were affected by the British. The aggression and conflict, caused by these shifts in culture, society and power well, is illustrated with the contradiction and struggle of the Ibo people, especially the protagonist Okonkwo in the second half of the novel. It is true that the arrival of the British slowly began to deteriorate the traditional Ibo society by using their religious and cultural strategy, but the greatest pitfall was to intervene in tribal disputes according to their own way rather than allowing the Ibo to settle issues in a traditional manner. The primary intention of the colonizers was to have full control over the territory of Ibo culture. So they disguised themselves as reformers and developer of society, which is affected by prejudices and bad practices.

Achebe tries to bring to our view the disintegration of culture in *Things Fall Apart*. The devastation in culture is categorized based on customs of the natives, religion and government. The story begins with a vivid description of the protagonist Okonkwo. Achebe is very particular in bringing a deep insight into the culture. Through the characters Okoye and Unoka, he tries to bring to our view how the clan and the title of the clan are important to every man of Ibo culture. This is well depicted in the first chapter of *Things Fall Apart*:

When Unoka died he had taken no title at all and he was heavily in debt. No wonder then that his son Okonkwo was ashamed of him....To crown it all he had taken two titles and had shown incredible prowess in two inter-tribal wars. And so although Okonkwo was still young, he was already one of the greatest men of his time. Age was respected among his people, but achievement was revered" (TFA, 6).

Achebe has utilized the organic structure of the novel to express the true picture of his land and the people. He has projected the African as an individual with infinite possibilities and has transmitted the socio-economic, political and cultural network of Igbos from the African perspective into the artistic genre of the novel. (Jai Ram, 1). *Things Fall Apart* is divided into three parts. The first part deals with Okonkwo, his people, his culture and his sacrifice of his for the rituals that he has to follow and his accidental murder of a boy of his land. The second part deals with Okonkwo's exile to his mother country Mbanta. The third part deals with his return to Umuofia and his care towards his culture and society that he sacrifices his own life to keep up the goodwill of his culture and Igbo people.Okonkwo, the protagonist, typifies the Igbo society to a large extent. He is an excellent individual, a fine product of a society, the culture of which demands unquestioning loyalty to the clan's ethnic in daily existence. His decisiveness and dauntless will are enough evidence of the impact of his society's culture on him. (Jayalaksmi, 12) Ernest Emenyonu says that the European colonial enterprise in Nigeria and the rest of Africa was decidedly geared towards the total eradication of the African cultural heritage and its replacement with the western (eurocentric) culture. (29)

Things Fall Apart portrays the clan which suffers the entry of the White man, They enter so as to civilize but bring chaos in every behaviour of the people. *Things Fall Apart* is an African novel because it aptly mirrors the African sensibilities, culture and worldview, while specifically relying on Igbo cosmology to attain its objectives. It does this by exploring core aspects of the Igbo traditions and customs at the threshold of the European colonization or intervention in the internal affairs of the Igbo. (Emenyonu and Nnolim, 32)

"In Okonkwo's society, a man is judged by his worth and not according to his father" (TFA, 92). This comment by the narrator shows that Okonkwo's people, by their culture, recognize personal identity and personal achievement. Achebe specifies that the destruction of an individual gives rise to the destruction in his culture. *Things Fall Apart* brings to us Okonkwo the protagonist who suffers from an identical crisis in order to balance him with his family to a new form of civilization and his own identity. According to him, a man's fame is decided by his valour and his position in the clan. To him, nothing is more important than holding high the name of the clan. Achebe buttresses the fact of personal achievement being revered in Igbo culture with the use of an apt proverb. The narrator says that "If a child washed his hands he could eat with kings", Okonkwo had clearly washed his hands and so he ate with kings and elders" (6)

Achebe in his first novel *Things Fall Apart* beautifully leads us through the transition. "Gikandi sees the novel as asserting the validity of African culture and its concepts of time and being, but he does so well aware of the fact that the Igbo world in the novel is mediated by the novelist's sources, both Igbo and colonial" (Whitaker, Msiska, 73). Thus, for example, after introducing the fact of Nwoye's apostasy and after depicting for several pages the first encounter between the Christian missionaries and the Igbo's, Achebe returns to Nwoye's conversion with the following sentences: 'But there was a young lad who had been captivated [by Christianity]"(Whitaker, Msiska 88). The Igbo culture lays a great deal of emphasis on differences, on dualities, on otherness. This is why we do not find it difficult to accept that other people somewhere else might be doing one thing differently from ourselves.

Chinua Achebe in *Things Fall Apart* represents the cultural roots of the Ibos in order to provide self-confidence, but at the same time, hc refers them to universal principles which vitiate their destructive potential. (Rhoads, 61) Achebe does not believe in what is called the 'rich material civilization' as said by Izevbaye. He wants to concentrate on the humanistic aspect of it To him *Things Fall Apart* is packed with human emotions and human conflicts and his main aim is to portray thc "Igbo as isolated and individual, evolving their own "humanistic civilization" (Rhoads, 62). Even violence internal to the culture is often conceptualized in terms of ethnocentric distinctions between insiders and outsiders, borders and border crossings. (Hogberg, 69). Even the Igbos virtues tell against them in the breaking of the clan. Their tolerance of the missionaries allowed the Christians to get a foothold in the villages. Their law against killing another member of the clan prevents them from killing the converts to Christianity. (Rhoads, 69)

Achebe clearly delineates the structure and the rituals of the Igbo society, and furthermore, he makes clear that the Igbo had a rich culture in themselves and it is not necessary for the British to come and civilize them. The clan were well organized and the people were appreciated for their good endeavours and also punished for their bad deeds. They had customs that would benefit the society rather than disturb or create havoc in the society. One of the customs was breaking the peace of Ani. (TFA, 24)

The punishment was very dreadful for those who failed to follow peace. The person was dragged to the bare ground until he was dead. The practice was stopped because it had no logic; it spoiled the peace of the weak either way.

Irele observes that the culture of Umuofia as depicted by Achebe functions through the immanence of its foundation myth in the collective life and consciousness. (122) The myth is treated in a vivid manner and the importance of it is felt in every manner and the action of the natives. The people believe themselves in the ancestral spirits and they think that they are evoked when something goes wrong in society. Irele sees *Things Fall Apart* "The reconstruction of Ibo village life is directed at revealing the forces at work both inside and outside traditional society that prepared the way for its eventual disintegration" (Whitaker, Msiska, 60).

Such wonderful memories and practices are totally sacked from the native people through Christianity. It was not only Christianity but the impact of colonization and slave trade that had brought drastic changes in the Igbo society. Though Africa had been witnessing colonization in various segments, it was through Christianity that people and the culture were transformed. Achebe portrays the destruction of culture through the three generations in his first three novels, and, the transformation is subjective to the identical crisis, the disintegration of culture and distortion of customs and rituals.

When the missionaries first arrived in Mbanta they witnessed a very rigid group of people and the Igbo people witnessed the white man had an authoritative or a dominant voice which led the Igbo people to obey and listen to his words. The foremost point that the missionaries insisted on was the Igbo were all under the evil curse of heathen worship and God has sent the missionaries to save them from the curse. Heathenism was the core component of the Igbo culture and this was the start of cultural destruction. The Missionaries were very stern towards stopping the heathen worship. The Igbo people were in a dilemma and asked “If we leave our gods and follow your god, who will protect us from the anger of our neglected gods and ancestors?" (TFA, 107)

Enoch the son of the snake priest was overexcited with the new religious rituals. He considered it adventurous and adapted different ways in proving that his conversion as a Christian has brought power and protection of the heathen god. Christianity has proved to be wrong in such cases wherein the convert started exploiting and abusing his native customs and his rituals. For example, it is believed that Enoch the son of the snake priest has killed and eaten a python which is considered a great abomination in the eyes of the custom. The leaders of Christianity are not courteous enough to tell the converts not to disturb the culture. In fact, the church enjoyed seeing its members becoming aggressive against their native people and their custom. Such a condition arose when Enoch unmasked the Egwugwu the ancestral spirit in the public. The Igbo people no longer cherished their culture or its beliefs. They were overwhelmed by their new religion and its customs. Achebe has crafted characters like Enoch to signify the cultural disintegration due to colonization.

In the name of civilization, the colonizer destroyed a community of rich heritage and culture. A traditional society is destroyed by the encroachment of outside civilization. Christianity in society has transformed the people and its community which was to be believed to be protected by the ancestral gods of different forms. The fear of God and their ancestors are totally exploited and the culture and the civilization of the natives are completely collapsed. The white man is ruthless and efficient, whereas the natives are weak and not able to withstand the outside force.

The notion of Rose Fall Apart is the historical reconstruction of a lost civilization that, despite inherent flaws that will eventually be the nuclei of its destabilization, was friendly and welcoming to strangers – qualities that worked ultimately to its disadvantage. (17) "Achebe reveals that the Europeans' ideas of Africa are mistaken. Perhaps the most important mistake of the British is their belief that all civilization progresses, as theirs has, from the tribal stage through monarchy to parliamentary government" (Rhoads, 63)

Civilization should transform the individual for the betterment of society and its people. Achebe's novels focus that the dawn of civilization that has doomed the Igbo culture and its roots. In *Things Fall Apart* and its sequel, Achebe traces the transition that colonization has wrought over the Igbo culture and its beliefs. A man can never live in a dual culture. If he should live peacefully he should either adapt or detach from it, which was indeed impossible. Dualism—two societies, separate and unequal—was a strategy of underdevelopment. The underdevelopment of local society was not simply an effect but an objective of colonial "development". Dualism, or the double standard, was never intended to "preserve traditions, as was claimed, but to destroy native society." (Giovanucci, 54). Thus was the native society and its beliefs were killed and molested by the arrival of Christianity. Colonization brought only slaves wherein Christianity brought believers.

In the name of heathenism, the Europeans entered into every wing they could. The natives were ignorant according to them and they needed a god who would save them in times of danger. When they came to know that they were washed from their sins they very much obliged to the religion. Colonialism could not be reformed into a "just" system of patronage and "protection". The creation of a just society necessarily entailed the destruction of colonial "patronage" (Giovunucci, 59).

Critics like Nichols, Traore and Lubiano in Lindfords 1991 have noted that one of Achebe's aims is to present the peculiarities of the Igbo culture, especially the beauties and wisdom of its art and institutions, though, Achebe also presents its weaknesses which require change and which aid in its destruction. (Rhoads, 61) Though *No Longer at Ease* is the second novel of Achebe, the continuity of the lost tradition is portrayed in his third novel *Arrow of God* in Achebe's trilogy. "As a proud winner of the coveted Jack Campbell New Statesman Award, *Arrow of God* is described as the magnum opus of Achebe. Admittedly one of his best books, and undoubtedly his favourite as evidenced by the fact that it is *Arrow of the God* that Achebe is often caught sitting with, it is the sequel to *Things Fall Apart* in more ways than one" (Vempala, 48).

"Disputes in pre-colonial Africa were primarily a result of various conflicts of interests such as breach of contract, slander, accusations of witchcraft, marital misunderstandings, injuries against persons and damage to property. Conflict could also occur between communities over problems of determining ownership rights over natural resources or territorial boundaries" (Mensah Fred, 137). Such was the fight between Umuaro and Okperi in *Arrow of God.* These were menial wars but they portrayed the strength, union and valour of the clan and its members Umaroa comprises six villages Umuachala, Umunneora, Umuagu, Umuezeani, Umuogwugwu and Umuisiuzo.

Then the hired soldiers of Abam used to strike in the dead of the night, set fire to the houses to carry men, women and children into slavery. Things were so bad for the six villages that their leaders came together to save themselves. They hired a strong team of medicine men to install a common deity for them. This deity which the fathers of the six villages made was called Ulu. The six villages then took the name of Umuroa and the priest of Ulu became their Chief Priest. (AOG 15)

Achebe has brought to our focus *Arrow of God* as a novel that deliberates to us the natives' transformation of their culture and disintegration. The natives are very much aware of the change as well as the danger that lay in front of them. Chief Priest of Ulu is Ezeulu whereas Eze in Igbo means king so Ezeulu was the priest-king of the six villages. Ezeulu is the man of wisdom and he is quite aware that the knowledge and the wisdom of the White man are more important in order to develop his country and attain material prosperity. For this reason, he sends his son to know the ways of the white man and also said that if there is nothing he can come back. But if there is something in the religion Ezeulu asked his son Uduche to bring home his share.

Captain Winter bottom unlike other colonial administrators is quite convinced about his mission in Africa. For "His strong belief in the value of the British mission in Africa was, strangely enough, strengthened during the Cameroon campaign of 1916" (AOG, 31) The slow transition of the Igbo people is beautifully painted by Achebe. In the conversation between Winter Bottom and his servant, John the transition of the language of the native people is perfectly shown by Achebe. The children of the village were playing in the rain and the captain asked John whether all those children are his. For that, he replied: "No, sir, said John putting down the chair and pointing. " My pickin na dat two wey de ru yonder and that yellow gal. Di oder two na Cook im pickin. Di oder yonder na Gardener him brodder pickin" (AOG, 32). Achebe has presented the Igbo inflicted English in the *Arrow of God* and showed that the native instead of having an interpreter started to learn the English language, but their hard tongue would not let the pronunciation right through.

The killing of the royal python seemed to have been an adventurous task of the Igbos because Enoch had the passion of killing a royal python which is considered an abomination in their tribe. In the same way, Oduche also tries to kill the royal python, but he did not have the courage to kill it. He closed it in a box and let it die of suffocation. Christian preachers like Mr Good Country insisted that python is a symbol of disgrace, temptation and disobedience though converts like Moses protested that the python did not harm the people in any way. Mr Good country told the converts of Umuarao "If we are Christians, we must be ready to die for faith' 'You must be ready to kill the python as the people of the rivers killed the iguana. You address the python as a father. It is nothing but a snake, the snake that deceived our first mother. If you are afraid to kill it do not count yourself a Christian" (AOG, 48). This induced Oduche to kill the royal python.

The killing of the royal python seemed to have been an adventurous task of the Igbos because Enoch had the passion of killing a royal python which is considered an abomination in their tribe. In the same way, Oduche also tries to kill the royal python, but he did not have the courage to kill it. He closed it in a box and let it die of suffocation. Christian preachers like Mr Good Country insisted that python is a symbol of disgrace, temptation and disobedience though converts like Moses protested that the python did not harm the people in any way. Mr Good country told the converts of Umuarao "If we are Christians, we must be ready to die for faith' 'You must be ready to kill the python as the people of the rivers killed the iguana. You address the python as a father. It is nothing but a snake, the snake that deceived our first mother. If you are afraid to kill it do not count yourself a Christian" (AOG, 48). This induced Oduche to kill the royal python.A memorandum sent to Captain Winterbottom by the Lieutenant Governor revealed the purpose of the Colonial civilization. It said:

"My purpose in these paragraphs is limited to impressing on all Political Officers working among the tribes who lack the natural rulers of the necessity of developing without any further delay an effective system of " Indirect rule " based on the native intuitions." "To many colonial nations native administration means government by white men. You are all aware that H.M.G considers policy 153 mistaken. In place of the alternative of governing directly through administrative officers, there is the other method of trying while we endeavour to purge the native system of its abuses to build a higher civilization upon the soundly rooted native stock that had its foundation in the hearts and minds and the thought of the people and therefore on which we can more easily build, moulding it and establishing it into lines consonant with modern ideas and higher standards, and yet all the time enlisting the real force of the spirit of the people, instead of killing all that out and trying to start afresh. We must destroy the African atmosphere, the African mind, the whole foundation of his race...." (AOG, 57).

The memorandum by the Lieutenant Governor declared clearly the purpose of the colonial government. Their plan of action is to destroy completely the race and its roots itself in order to civilize them. The colonial government thinks that the native customs, rituals and practices are that which stands as a stumbling block for their development. "The great tragedy of British colonial administration was that the man on the spot who knew his African and knew that he was talking about found himself being constantly overruled by the star-eyed fellows at Headquarters" (58).

The European Colonization leads the natives like James Ikedi the Warrant Chief of Okperi to tax his own people. The European officers went to the extent of sleeping with the native women, and the cherished culture of the Igbo tradition and its chastity was being looted and demolished by the Colonial officers. Likewise native chiefs like James Ikedi "took any woman who caught his fancy without paying the customary bride price" (AOG, 58). It was the beginning of the devastation. Though James Ikedi was the first man to receive the mission education, it did not bring any bright and exuberant changes in him. Indeed it brought changes that led him to dominate his own people. One of the greatest misleading for the colonization is that it led the natives to a situation that made them feel that, with authority and the knowledge obtained by the colonial government and the mission schools, they can prosper in their life. This false notion of James Ikedi led him to tax his own people. The natives were inflicted by the colonizers' power and behaviour. Subsequently, they were lost in limbo and were unaware that through taxing their people they are the ones creating more devastation among the natives.

James Ikedi is considered to be the first cultured, civilized, intelligent man suffering from such a psychological imbalance due to the transition. As Manon observes, it is a dependency complex. He wants to be called himself a king, "so that he was now called His Highness Ikedi First, Obi of Okperi. This among a people who abominated kings! This was what the British administration was doing among the Ibos, making a dozen mushroom kings grow where there were none before" (59-60). The white man is busy planning his diplomatic moves to bring his civilization to the backward races. Captain Winter Bottom plans to appoint Ezeulu as the paramount chief of Umuaro.

Most of the characteristics and administration tactics of the Europeans also contributed to the devastation and ignorance of the native people. Mr Wright was forced to complete the road between Okperi and Umurao for which he initiated unpaid labour. These kinds of activities induced the native officer to follow the colonizers just the same way. They were ignorant of the danger that awaited behind such behaviour.

Resistance was one of the major characteristics that created great clashes between the colonizers and society. Mr Wright was very harsh in treating the natives. Sometimes he went to the extent of whipping them very badly. As a result of it, the natives began to show resistance toward such kind of treatment. One situation is when Obika the son of Ezeulu came to work fully drunk and induced laughter among the natives. Obika's behaviour was also kind of bullying Mr Wright. In an instance, Mr Wright took his whip and slashed Obika down. These kinds of clashes started creating more havoc among the society and the natives were at stake. The rigid behaviour of the Colonizers provoked the natives to resist them. In *Arrow of God*, violence is also hinted at. Whenever the issue of resistance is brought up, the answer is given that it would be a rash act. When the young men of Umuaro were inclined towards the decision that they would no longer work on the white men's road, they were told that their elders would be taken to prison at Okperi. (Nwoga, 34) Moses Unachukwu understood the danger that lay behind their resistance and he said "As daylight chases away the darkness so will the white man driveway all our customs. I know that as I say passes by your ears, but it will happen. The white man has power which comes from the true God and it burns like fire" (AOG, 86).

The implementation of certain policies by the European colonial government took a long way to reach the people, and due to the delay the policies were not fulfilled and the colonizers were not able to work. Due to the psychological pressure of imbalance between the natives and their government they became aggressive towards the natives. Clark the Assistant District Officer defines the difference between the French and the British Colonial administration. The French made up their minds about what they wanted to do and did it. The British, on the other hand never did anything without first sending out a Commission of Inquiry to discover all the facts, which then hamstrung them." Due to this kind of enquiry commission, the officers were forced to explore many things and that led to chaos among the people and its society.

It is clear, however, that it was not only the fear of violence that attracted the Igbo people of Umuaro to submission; new avenues to wealth and greatness was also part of it. Oduche is shown to have overcome reluctance to go to school because he was impressed with the knowledge of his first teacher Mr Molokwu, who could speak to the white man in his language of Mr Blackett, the West missionary was said to have more knowledge than even white man, of his later teacher Mr Goodcountry from the Delta who "spoke the white man's language as if it was his own" (AOG, 48)

Captain Winterbottom recommends Ezeulu as the Paramount Chief and deep down in his heart, he is angry with his government and its policies. To him, the commissions are unimportant things that hinder the development of colonial rule. He submits by telling that "The fault of our administration is that they invariably appoint the wrong people and set aside the advice of those of us who have forgotten for years" (110). According to Clarke, the commissions are useless and facts rule and domination is only superstitious rather than practical. Such kind of chaos among the European Government brought instability in a native country which resulted in a lot of chaos.

The reason for the devastation according to Ezeulu is the men in his own country. Ezeulu said "With all their powers and the magic white man would not have overrun entire Olu and the Igbo if we did not help them.... We showed them and are still showing them. ... We have shown the white man the way to go to our house and give him a stool to sit on. If we now want him to go away again we must either wait until he is tired of his visit or we must drive him away" (AOG, 133).

To Ezeulu colonization is "A disease that has never been seen before and it cannot be cured with everyday herbs." (134) and he also justifies that his son is sent to know the religion of the white man and it is moreover a sacrifice. Though Ezeulu desires the friendship of the white man, his enemies fail to perceive that he is not given worldly temptations and that therefore it is not surprising that he refuses the offer of the warrant chief. (Vempala, 60)Ezeulu would have been an unblemished embodiment of culture, in whom knowledge and compassion meet and constitute a rare blend if he had remained untouched by the many cares and causeless quarrels of his world. He misinterprets his own mental fixation as a dishonour dealt with him and his deity makes him dogmatic. And once he thus 158 becomes the victim of his own individualistic and impulsive nature, the interests of his society recede in his view, and, he is no more dynamic in action, no more capable of perception. (64)

Nwaka is not surprised to know that the white ruler had sent an invitation to Ezeulu, and he also does not appreciate Ezeulu for refusing the invitation, because he insists that Ezeulu is already the white ruler's friend. Nwaka then told about the danger of having a friendship with the white man as "any man who brings ant–ridden faggots into his hut should expect the visit of the lizards" (AOG, 145). Nwaka also insists that if Ezeulu is tired of the white man's friendship, he should remove his own knot and there is no contribution of the society and its people in that. Nwaka said "*You tied the knot, you should know how to undo it, you passed the shit that is smelling, you should carry it away*" (145)

The unity among the people was thoroughly destroyed due to the arrival of the white men and his government. In spite of knowing that the white man would not call a native man without a reason, Nwaka and the other members are in no way bothered and they react in such a way that Ezeulu is the sole responsibility for the white man's arrival in Umurao. After the arrest of Ezeulu, his compound was doomed and though it was the planting season the people in his Obi did not work. The Colonizers' policy of indirect rule started culminating in the hearts and the behaviour of the people. The people of Umurao were not ready to listen to anybody, not even their chief priest. As a result of it, the bond of their culture is totally demolished and it paved way for the white rulers and it made it easy for them to exploit the very foundation of their culture as said in the memorandum of the Governor.

People of Okperi have already started to work for the white man, and one followed the other. Nwabueze said that he came to Okperi to learn a dance and found that Ekemezie was no longer the dancer and instead he has joined the white man for work. The people were astonished to experience the benefits of jobs and money provided by the white man and so they gave up dancing and started to work for the white man. The impact of money-making is felt in the words of Ekemezie when he told Nwabueze "to leave dancing and join the race for the white man's money" and also said that everything was good in its season; dancing in the season of dancing. But he said, "a man of sense does not go on hunting little bunch rodents when his age mates are after the big game" (170). The natives were racing towards making money for the white man. Ekemezie also insisted to Nwabueze that "the race of the white man's money would not wait" (171). Nwabueze said that he also joined the race. Achebe sculpts the destruction of the native land through various characters. Ezeulu allowed his son to the white man's religion so that he would have an eye there, and also he wants his son to acquire the wisdom of the white man which will lead him to material prosperity. Nwabueze went to work for the white man to make money and to begin a small trade as soon as he had made some money. So, as discussed in the previous chapters, the destruction started within the individual and then lead to the destruction of their culture. It is the individual who accepts transition first. Eventually, the members of transition join and they destroy the cultural symbols of the nation. The people regretted that they are not able to amass wealth. Titles and fights of valour no longer had importance. They wanted to be wealthy and be a part of the white man's government.

Achebe also depicts some cultural problems like favouritism, laziness, tardiness and disunity among the villagers of the Ibo nation. The Igbo culture lost its uniqueness in the course of time. In 1868, bonny traditional religion declined, the previously sacred iguanas were killed, and by 1880s, the temple of skulls dedicated to war god, Ikuba was falling into ruins. Achebe Over –emphasizes the fact that inspite of the problems that the Igbo society experienced, before coming of the Europeans, it stood as a nation. But the arrival of the white man, 'Gyres of Anarchy' displaced the native societies and changed the Igbo's perception of culture. (Pandey, 33)

Achebe has brought to our view that colonization has changed the basic nature of the Igbo people. The majority of the Igbo were not interested in the transition that took place among the natives, and so they showed resistance towards the religion, the government and its policies. Too much resistance brought great destruction and disaster to the individual, the society and its culture. When Ezeulu resisted, Chief Clarke is in a dilemma to punish him or to let him free. Because once Ezeulu is let free "the reputation of the administration would sag to the ground especially in Umuaro where things were only now beginning to look after a long period of hostility to the administration and

Christianity.... Umuaro had put up more resistance to change than any other clan in the whole province" (AOG, 179).

The confrontation of Ezeulu with the white rulers and their government had no gain because the people never understood that their Chief Priest was denying such a great offer for the welfare of Umuaroa. Instead, characters like Nwaka said, "The man is proud as a lunatic. This proves what I have always told people, that he inherited his mother's madness" (178).

The white rulers and their administration is stuck in a very dilemmatic position on how to handle the natives. A letter by the Lieutenant Governor stated that the matter of appointing a Warrant Chief should be handled "with tact so that the Administration did not confuse the minds of the natives or create the impression of indecision or lack of direction as such an impression would do harm" (183). This tactfulness and cunningness were quite lacking in Ezeulu the chief priest. He believed the people so much and he thought that the people would understand his plans of sending his son to the white man's religion and rejecting the offer of the Warrant Chief. However, the disbelief and distrust of the people towards the chief priest have led to the destruction of Ezeulu and paved the way to the success of Christianity. Ezeulu's revenge is the core component that led to the exploitation of the traditional values as well as the destruction of their traditional religion. Ogbuefi Ofoka, in his visit to Ezeulu's hut after his return, proclaimed that it was only Ezeulu who could confront and wrestle with the Englishmen and he also insisted in his speech that the people of Umuaro were confused and it was Ezeulu himself who confused them. He said, "We are like the puppy in the proverb which attempted to answer two calls at once and broke its jaw" (AOG, 190). Ofoks also argues that it was Ezeulu who insisted on joining hands with the white man a few years back and it is he now again who "tells us to go and challenge the same white men" (190). Likewise, many situations reverberated the devastation that is caused and to is caused by the native's relation with the white men.

Ezeulu's revenge towards the natives broke apart the beauty and the ethics of the traditional Igbo society. The New Yam Festival was celebrated as the beginning of the new and the end of the old year. Achebe symbolically represented the New yam festival as the end of traditional values, rituals and celebrations and the beginning of the colonial rule. Because the prominent person who should announce the New Yam festival was now on the verge of taking revenge, as a consequence of it the white man's religion took its flight towards capturing the beliefs of the native people.

Ezeulu's anger and his passion and rigidness brought destruction to Umuaro. Ezeulu told that it was not his decision but the decision of the Ulu. He is not ready to break the rituals that had been followed for generations. Though the leaders of Umuaro told Ezeulu to eat the rest of the yams, and they would bear the consequence of it, Ezeulu never concedes to it. Onenyi blames the white ruler for the devastation. The leaders think that the devastation caused in the country is due to the arrest of the Chief Priest. Onenyi requested Ezeulu to find some solution to the problem and also brought to his view certain practices of their tribe changed in course of time.

Colonization had brought a great transition in the minds of the people especially in the Chief Priest of Ulu. He resists not eating the yams but he breaks the custom of sending his son to another religion. He was appointed as the Chief

Preist of Ulu in order to protect his village from destruction, but he became the key to destruction. Achebe delineated the destruction of the Igbo and their culture through Ezeulu. Ezeulu's denial of eating the Yam brought a great drop in the economic condition of Umuaro and people raged in anger against the Ezeulus. There was great alarm in the village of Umurao. "Meanwhile the rains thinned out. There was one last heavy down-pour to usher in a new moon. It brought down harmattan as well, and each new day made the earth harder so that the eventual task of digging up whatever remained of the harvest grew daily" (212).

The disagreement of Ezeulu had brought the whole village to witness their own annihilation. The colonizers were cunning and they planned each and every step that they took ahead, though they persuaded them to follow the religion in order to get civilized and cultured. Ezeulu was not cunning enough to have his people under control this led people to criticize the Ulu itself. The people said "A priest like Ezeulu leads a god to ruin himself, It has happened before.' Or perhaps a god-like Ulu leads a priest to ruin himself' (215).

The postponement brought great calamities to the village and many suffered. The great sufferer was Ogbuefi Amalu "who died in the rainy season from aru-mmo" (219). One of the greatest tragedies was that he before his death discussed with his sons to plan the burial feast a day or two after his death. Even then they were not able to arrange the feast due to the famine in their land. They had to borrow yam from their nearby land and "Many of the neighbouring clans were already growing fat out of Umuaro's misfortune. Every Nkwo market brought new yams to Umuaro and sold them like anklets of ivory" (220)

Thus it was the beginning of the disintegration of culture, which led even a stern man like Nwaka who resisted the white man, his religion and his school to bend a little and send his son to school. Famine raged against the Ulu itself. Just like the saying of Ezeulu's ancestors, 'when brothers fight to the death a stranger inherits their father's estate' (222). This was the condition of Umuaro, "the church was offering sanctuary to those who wished to escape the vengeance of Ulu" (222).

The system and the beauty of the tradition were contaminated, and people were ready to offer sacrifice to the church in order to escape their harvest. It was the intruding of the white men that brought such transition in the minds of the people. And converts like Moses Unachukwu added to the destruction and explained that "If Ulu who is false god can eat one yam, the living God who owns the whole world should be entitled to eat more than one" (218).

Umuaro witnessed the destruction of its clan, "the clan which long, long ago when lizards were in ones and twos chose his ancestors to carry their deity and go before them challenging every obstacle and confronting every danger on their behalf" (222). Such beliefs of the people were totally ruined and vanquished from the mind of the people.Even after the announcement of the New Yam Festival, Ezeulu was not relieved from his burden and the death of Obika was considered as a punishment for Ezeulu, who brought devastation for his people and upon himself. Achebe's *Arrow of God* is a powerful novel because it shows that the immense power of colonialism can cripple even the strongest of men like Ezeulu. While we watch Ezeulu spending the remainder of his waning life living "in the haughty splendour of a demented high priest" spared the knowledge of the final outcome, a question forms in our minds: If Ezeulu could not stand up to the white man, what chance did the average man have? (232)

Nwoga observes that the desertion of Ulu arose from these internal problems. The Christian mission was present in Umuaro as part of the external influence, but it was still peripheral. Neither Christianity nor Ulu worship is presented as a theological system; neither is presented with a mythology that is much in evidence. They are both cultural and social factors and one replaces the other in a survival state.Just as the Memorandum stated, the culture, tradition and the gods were uprooted by the white man's religion and the man who fought to protect his traditions and customs stood aside like a dead man. The people who protested that Ezeulu was the reason for the white man's arrival, accepted the religion and obeyed its rituals. "Finally, there is the Christian missionary enterprise that works as a middle ground between the priest and of the Igbo society and the colonial administration" (Pandey, 68).

Many countries in transition suffer from chronic and systemic corruption that compromises governance and slows economic growth. Bribery, corruption's principal manifestation, is as old as recorded history and is even mentioned in Psalm of David 15 as one of those basic volitional actions that will prevent one from "dwelling upon Thy holy mountain" (Spector, 24). The concept of bribery is the core component and the base of Achebe's *No Longer at Ease*. "Achebe shows the impact of western education and the culture on the Igbos, especially the youth. Achebe reflects the problem of corruption in 1950s Lagos. The carving for money and other material possessions promoted corruption in the Igbo society" (Pandey, 37). Achebe in his second Novel *No Longer at*

Ease attempts to analyze the contemporary society that suffers due to imperialist's slavery and colonization. Obi Okonkwo stands a rigid example of a man who completely lost himself to the imperialist's power, position and way of living.

Mercedes discusses that "Bribery is something particularly disgusting to the British now that the corrupt days of Samual Pepys are sufficiently in the past. This book does not condone bribery but explains it. The book exposes the "road "to the public gaze, which is surely the first step towards its destruction. Only an African writer could do this with such devastating effect" (550). The Nigerian society was preparing itself for corruption. "As the hero of Achebe's story, Obi reveals how the use of cultural assimilation of colonial Nigeria contradicts to a large extent the aim of its outspoken defenders in the circle of Christian missionaries and educators. He admits like Achebe himself the gross error of Europeans in Africa" (Babalola, 140).

One of the greatest drawbacks of Nigerian society was that they were easily influenced by the European powers. Achebe specifies certain characteristics in each of his characters that led to the disintegration of their traditional society. Achebe in No Longer traces the next level of disintegration of the Igbo society. The religion, the education and the menial jobs which were spouting in his previous novels have grown to establish its rule in the society. As a result, the natives decided to send their intelligent son of the country to study abroad. "They taxed themselves mercilessly" (NLE, 6) for educating the son of the soil. Achebe strikes the core idea of disintegration in Nigerian society. Contemporary society was governed by western ideas. Society was all set to go aspiring their development in the western society. The atmosphere was fully colonized. Christianity was followed at home, and people sent their children to schools and also abroad for well-paid jobs and to step ahead towards modern living.

People of the Nigerian society were completely bound with superstitious beliefs and worshipped ancestral spirits, animals and nature as Gods. *No Longer at Ease* portrays a society that has already lost its traditional values under the spell of the white government and education and its job abroad. The deterioration of Igbo culture and its beliefs could be observed through the speech of Reverend Samuel Ikedi of St Mark's Anglican Church. He told that: In the times past, ... Umuofia would have required of you to fight in her wars and bring home human heads. But those were the days of darkness from which we have been delivered by the blood and the Lamb of God. Today we send you to bring knowledge. Remember the fear of the Lord is the beginning of Wisdom" (NLE, 8).

Achebe's great and deep passion for mutation has been greatly portrayed in the novel *No Longer at Ease*. The breaking of the kola nut is no longer a cherished practice. Hymns and prayers fulfilled the purpose of worship. The new religion has warned the people who worshipped pagan gods. They treated the Igbo gods as mere idols. The people in order to move their life towards modernity forgot their tradition and started observing the new religion and its ethics.

The white man's culture has induced great curiosity in the mind of the youngsters like Joseph Okeke who works as a clerk in the survey department. Joseph told Obi about the cinema, dance halls and political meetings. He also added that "Dancing is very important nowadays. No girl will look after you if you can't dance."(NLE 11). The people were camouflaged with western culture. The masks that they carried for preserving the traditional values are now replaced with the mask of modern living. They were totally lost. “Obi was fascinated by what he was learning of the sinful world.’ (11)

“ Whether or not the quid pro quo in fact occurs after the corrupt transaction is initiated depends upon the ethics, desperation, desire for gratification and fear of punishment of both sides in the transaction” (Spector, 24). As Spector states corruption is more than just a function of personal greed or cultural predisposition. (24) *No Longer at Ease* is moved exactly as per the observation of Lyons. It is not only personal greed but more than that. For instance, bribery became a basic quality of many of the Nigerian public. It was over the flow in Nigerian public life. Corruption began from the scarp to the creamy layer. In a conversation between Christopher and Obi, Achebe illustrates that the natives were raised to a high position through bribes. According to Obi’s factual analysis, “The Civil Service is corrupt because of these so-called experienced men at the top" (NLE, 16). Achebe also specified through conversation that bribery was a natural process for very old people. Bribery was considered a continuous process or a cycle. The man who gave the bribe, received it when it was his turn.

The people have lost their senses and are insane towards making money through the men acquired knowledge and placed in government positions. They were still barbaric in their thought and actions. The majority of the people were selfish and they led astray their land and their culture and its importance and moved behind the crowd which taught them how to make money and exploit the name of their culture. The conversation between obi and Christopher categorized the people into three types. First are the experienced men at the top. Second, the people who had no problem with the bribe because they were raised to a position without bribing anyone. The third group of "the educated Nigerians had gone back to eating pounded yams or garri with their fingers for the good reason it tasted better that way. Also, for the even better reason that they were not as scared as the first generation of being uncivilized" (NLE, 16).

No Longer at Ease concentrates on these three types of people through whom the real devastation takes action. Obi has forgotten the purpose for which he has been sent abroad and fell in love. His love affair, which seemed to be a very petty issue, creates a great disaster in his life as well as in his relationship with the Umuofia Progressive Union. Colonization is deep-rooted in the mind and the life of the common people, especially in educated youngsters like Obi Okonkwo.

Corruption has not astonished the people of Nigeria. Colonization did bring great disaster in the mind and the living of the Igbo people. But it was their own free 170 will that allowed the destruction. As discussed in the first chapter, the people suffered from what is called a dependency complex. Bribe became mandatory in the life of the colonized Igbo people. When Obi visits the Umuofia Progressive Union for the first time after he had completed his studies in London, The Secretary "told them about the value of education. "Education to service, not for white-color jobs and comfortable salaries. With our great threshold of independence, we need men who are prepared to serve her well and truly" (26). The Secretary's talk revolutionized Obi's heart but soon the spirit came totally down when the Vice President said "Those of you who know books will not have any difficulty. Otherwise, I would have suggested seeing some men beforehand" (26).

Hard work and self-confidence lacked in the people. Achebe portrayed in *No Longer at Ease* that the Nigerians were not responsible. Civilization brought laziness and they lost the responsibility of the development of their nation. According to Obi Okonkwo's theory "The public service of Nigeria would remain corrupt until the old Africans at the top were replaced by young men from the universities. In his interview, he witnessed three classic Africans who had no role in the interview. Two among them did not show any interest whereas the other slept throughout the interview. The Igbo society that is found in Achebe's first novel is completely vanquished. Society was *No Longer at Ease*. The people did not respond or get angry at any of the behaviour or taunts of the white government. If one needs a job he should be quiet. Obi called it 'colonial mentality'" (33).

"Where does one begin? With the masses? Educate the masses? It would take centuries. A handful of men at the top. Or even one man with a vision- an enlightened dictator. People are scared of the world nowadays. But what kind of democracy can exist side by side with so much corruption and ignorance? Perhaps a halfway house- a sort of compromise" (35). Bribe and ignorance hindered the development of the nation. The valour of questioning faded among the native people. The transition in the mind of the people could be observed through the words of Odogwu. He said, "Titles are no longer great, either barns or a large number of wives and children. Greatness is now in the things of the white man. And so we too have changed our tune" (43).

The European Government offered many privileges for the natives. After Obi joined the Civil Service, he was astonished by the benefits on the very first day. He was completely blindfolded and was not in the least worried about the debt that he had to clear for the Umuofia Progressive Union. Within a week he bought a Morris Oxford with the car advance and was also given sixty an outfit allowance. Obi from the very first day was lost in the comfort and the pleasures of the new world of uncertainty.

The Igbo people who lived in huts and the woman who covered the body with camwood, and the man who had a passion for hunting and fighting was not easy to find in the contemporary society of Nigeria. The European Government had really taken full control, just like the memorandum explained in *Arrow of God*. The Indirect Rule worked perfectly and the European government had the least difficulty in handling the people because they had their natives to control them. The Government built houses at the cost of thirty-five thousand each for the ministers.

Colonization stripped off the fear in the native people. They believed that the new religion, the government and its people would save them from the danger and anger of the ancestral spirits. They got rid of superstitious beliefs and were indeed strengthened by the doctrines of the Gospel. But these doctrines were not used in any way to build a nation, rather it was used personally. Obi is not very acquainted with Christianity or the colonial government but he uses its benefits whenever necessary. He decides to get married to Osu. Obi was against the practices and the age-old beliefs of his tribe. "The individual isolation of Obi Okonkwo is largely due to his own indecisive nature, and to a certain extent, his disadvantageous position. By belonging neither to the traditional Umofian culture, the values he started questioning as a result of his western education, nor to the Western culture, for his sentimental ties to his motherland proves rather tenacious, Obi feels alienated. And it is this alienation that accounts for his tragedy" (Vempala, 85).

It was the beginning of destruction both in the cultural values as well as the moral values of Obi. His love towards Clara and his decision to get married to an Osu led him to the path of destruction. The efficacy of the people was shrunken to mere laziness. The power and the luxury of the government job should have initiated great development in the individual. But the youngsters became extremely lazy. An example of a lazy youngster was "Joshua Udo, a messenger in the Post office, had been sacked for sleeping while on duty" (NLE, 62). Umuofia initially had been fighting for rights, land disputes and seeking recognition as well, but in the contemporary society, the youngsters were fighting "that they were not given any of the two bottles of beer which had been bought" (64) for the meeting of the Umuofia Progressive Union.

In *No Longer at Ease* Achebe's main motive is to bring about the transition that arose due to colonization. Bribery and corruption were the twin ideas that paved way for the destruction of the nation and its culture. Mr Mac arrived at Obi's office and was ready to bribe him for his sister's Federal Scholarship to study in England. The Colonizers thought that they have civilized Nigeria by providing education, government jobs and so on. But the truth is people involved themselves in getting and giving bribes. Elsie explains to Obi the process of getting and the reason for giving bribes. With a Grade One Certificate one stood a great chance to win the scholarship said, Obi. But it was countered by Elsie. Who told that it was not only important to impress the board, rather it was necessary to meet the members at home. The hypocritic behaviour of youngsters like Elsie forced them to go to any extent for receiving a scholarship. They no longer care about being a virgin or losing their chastity. Selfishness became their prime quality; they were rather dead as an Igbo and was reborn with the qualities of a westerner. They suffered from being not able to balance their change.

A university Degree was the philosopher's stone. It transmuted a third-class clerk on one hundred and fifty a year into a senior Civil Servant on five hundred and seventy, with the car and luxuriously furnished 174 quarters at a nominal rent. And the disparity in salary and amenities did not tell even half the story. To occupy a European post was second only to actually being a European. It raised a man from the masses of the elite whose small talk at the cock tail parties was 'How's the car behaving?' (NLE, 73).

These are the voices of the bereaved condition of the Igbo youngsters. They were devoid of the knowledge of understanding the real necessities for a happy life. They lived in the illusion of becoming a European after acquiring a university education and a Civil Service job. As Spector identifies, weak and ill-conceived incentives also make societies vulnerable to corruption—when civil servants are not paid a living wage, when there are few rewards for good performance, and when there is little fear of punishment for wrongdoing. (24) Obi's condition was much more like that. He had benefits that could not fit his stand, and moreover, he added more and more on his lavishness at the end of which he could not make both ends meet. Obi was getting furious over his commitments. He was also under the pressure to repay his scholarship to the Umuofia Progressive Union.

Finally, in developing countries where citizen loyalties to the state are still in a formative stage and maybe more strongly focused on personal, tribal or clan relationships, corruption in the state can grow because accountability is not enforced. (SPector24) Achebe in *No Longer at Ease* brings forth a society that is not in the least bothered about their country. The European government was making a big mistake in educating the Nigerians. As Mr Green puts it, "Education for what? To get as much as they can for themselves and their family. Not in the least bit interested in thc millions of their countrymen who die every day from hunger and diseases" (NLE, 93). The devastation of the culture de facto occurred not only because of the colonial, encounter but occurred in the manner they accepted and perceived the change. The change was utmost worse in the youngsters. The chastity and the culture of the tradition and its destruction can be deeply felt in the argument between Charles and Obi: "No man wants to part with his money. If you accept money from a man you make him poorer. But if you go to bed with a girl who asks for it, I don't see that you have done any harm" (97).

Christianity has brought great changes in the tradition and the culture of the native, but it never insisted that they should go against the law. It was an abomination to get married to an Osu, it meant dedication to god. The youngster revolted against their custom and tradition not for the sake of the betterment of the country, but for their own sake. In the Igbo tradition "Osu is like leprosy in the minds of the people. But all that is going to change. In ten years things will be quite different from what they are now" (107).

Isaac Okonkwo who was called Nwoye in Igbo left his father's house to join Christianity whereas his son Obi Okonkwo goes against his parents to get married to an Osu. Obi's father is the victim of the transition, as he is neither able to achieve and flourish in his tradition nor in the religion that he embraced. He very pathetically states: "I left my father's house, and he placed a curse on me. I went through fire to become a Christian. Because I suffered I understand Christianity – more than you will ever do" (110). These lines were quite emphatic of destruction that would come upon Obi. Obi is bound with the need for money for Clara's abortion, his brother's education, his mother's treatment and for his car's insurance. Obi is overwhelmed with sorrow.

It is Achebe who spoke through the character of Mr Green who criticizes the privileges given to the Nigerians. Mr Green is quite disturbed by the irresponsible behaviour of Mr Obi Okonkwo. He in his distress said "It's people like you who ought to make the Government decide. That is what I have always said. There is no single Nigerian who is prepared to forgo little privileges in the interests of his country, from your ministers down to your most junior clerk. And you tell me you want to govern yourselves" (122)

Achebe highlights the destruction at its top when Obi had lost in the world of money, love, sex, revolt and power and even resisted and felt ashamed to know that he in spite of holding a Civil Servant job could not develop his family. At the height of it is he denied going even to his mother's funeral. What has colonization wrought in the individual of the traditional Igbo society? A man scrambled and lost in his own culture. "That is what Lagos can do to a young man. He runs after sweet things, dances breast to breast with women and forgets his home and his people" (127).

Obi is the replica of the devastation poured upon youngsters due to colonization. Having lost his mother and Clara, Obi was blindfolded about the things happening around him. Lagos had taught him to dance, to love, to have sex, to betray, live a luxurious living with debts all around, and the significant things that Obi learned were to receive bribes. Colonization led the people in the middle of a dilemmatic transition. They could neither follow their culture nor neglect nor run away from the benefits that they embraced due to the change. Eventually, they submit themselves to the destruction of the change. Obi started getting bribes. "But Obi stoutly refused to countenance anyone who did not possess the minimum educational and other requirements. On that he was unshakeable" (135). "Obi was, without doubt, a very foolish and self–willed young man....that if you want to eat toad you should look for fat and juicy ones." It is all a lack of experience. The natives bribed their own people. Corruption and bribe were the prime factors that were promoted in the process of Colonization.

According to Spector corruption acts as counterproductive for development. He puts forth three main ideas that make corruption counterproductive. Firstly corruption impairs the possibilities of economic growth. It also hinders the benefits for the state and it encourages a shadow economy wherein the revenue is paid to the corrupt bureaucrats rather than to the state. Secondly, it reduces the power and a state's governing ability. The essence of public service is lost and the government treasury is looted into the pockets of the corrupt officials. Thirdly corruption demoralizes the public and results in a loss of confidence and trust in the government. "Corruption is an implicit and sometimes explicit, negotiated contract specifying what each party has committed itself to accomplish, that is, the quid pro quo" (30).

"The aftermaths of the Western takeover of the traditional African societies have had different effects on different individuals. Against a background of corruption and erosion of traditional values, the likes of Nanga live solely for themselves amassing wealth by plundering the nation" (Vempala, 114). "Government officials regularly taking commissions, percentages of the contract their departments awarded to private companies to build a road or a school, was a time-honoured tradition in Nigeria, almost human nature." (AMOP, vii).

The degeneration of moral values can be seen in M.A Nanga the protagonist of Achebe's novel A Man of the People, Chief Nanga has been shown as a corrupt politician who knew how to give and take bribes.... Europeans knew what the Igbo people wanted; they knew that without the help of the Igbos they could not disintegrate the society. That is the reason corruption was promoted and encouraged in modern Igbo society. (Pandey, 49)

Political unrest and reports of corruption among the government officials, known as the 'temper centres' for the amount they screamed off the top of contracts – again rather modest by today's standards – further discredited the political class in the eyes of many Nigerians. Mensah observes that like any human society the African communities had a lot of conflicts within themselves. "As Zartman noted, conflict is an inevitable aspect of human interaction, an unavoidable consequence of human decisions and choices" (137).

The history of Western development in the so-called underdeveloped world is, in large part, the history of colonialism. While colonialism embodied a broad range of phenomena, it may be noted that the "development" of local resources in the colonies and protectorates were central to the so-called "world market" dominated by the Western colonial powers. Local resources in the colonized world—e.g., sugar, coffee, tobacco, produce, spices, opium, minerals, rubber and eventually, oil and gas—were the point of the colonial system, all rationalizing ideologies—e.g., "manifest destiny," "civilizing mission"—aside. Colonial "development" entailed the intervention of the West into the political and economic autonomy of the colonized and "protected" nations and communities. (Giovanucci, 15)

"Modernization" gives way instead to cultural essentialism which displaces the history of development. In the absence of history, cultural essentialism arises to explain away the features of a chronically exploitative relationship between the "developed" and the "developing" nations. (16) Giovanucci identified that the measure of "progress" is defined by the presence of Western-style gadgets and systems. Whether "high tech" is conceived as Magnavox colour TVs or as global positioning networks is a relative matter. The West is yet perceived as the source of "state-of-the-art" modernity through association with its technological "signs" (19). Odili Samalu criticizes people who buy cars but later on, he is also stuck with the passion of getting a car, just as Giovanucci notes that progress is defined by westernized living as well as the use of westernized things and gadgets.

Within a decade of Man of the People's publication, Nigeria had become a major international oil producer, reaching the current position as the sixth bigger export among the members of the Organization of the Petroleum Exporting Countries. Nigeria had earned some $300 billion over the ensuing decades, with a very little show for it. Much of the money had been stolen, placed into Western bank accounts by the country's leaders, or siphoned off by contractors .As the retired General Ishola Williams, who works with the anti-corruption Organization Transparency International, puts it, the Nigerian state has become the 'a government of the contractors, by the contractors and for the contractors.' (Karl Meir, 2001).

The opening of Achebe's *Man of the People* is a lead to deduce the plot of the novel. The main reason for the devastation that occurred in the country was due to the 'Miscreant Gang of highly educated professional men' (MOP, 4). The article in The Daily Chronicle of an official organ of the POP was quite aggressive on the educated Nigerians because of their irresponsible, selfish, covetous behaviour. The article stated:

Let us now and for all the time extract from our body –politics as a dentist extracts a stinking tooth all those decadent stooges versed in textbook economics and aping white man's mannerisms and way of speaking. We are proud to be Africans. Our true leaders are not those intoxicated with their Oxford, Cambridge or Harvard Degrees but those who speak the language of the people. Away with the damnable and expensive university education which only alienates the African from his rich and ancient culture and puts him above his people. (MOP, 4)

Achebe in his novel A *Man of the People* has presented a society that was in a rush to acquire power and position in politics. Chief Nanga was a perfect embodiment of a jealous and selfish politician. Though he was once a teacher, he forgot the value and the cost of University education. He does not allow even the youngsters who are ready and duty conscious. To Chief Nanga, education was for amassing more wealth and acquiring status. He also wants the budding officers to yield to his advice and not to interfere in the perfection of any duty towards the country. A common saying after independence was that it didn't matter what you knew but who you knew" (15). Corruption and bribe hinder the development of the nation. A nation's revenue is looted by so-called politicians. Achebe in his first novel *Things Fall Apart* shows a tradition that was fighting in unity for its rights and also supporting the helpless people. The people had the freedom to develop. Though they were superstitious they were not blind to witness people in need. Such unity was lost due to colonization. After colonization people became selfish and narrow-minded. The youngsters concentrated only on themselves and their families. The reason that the natives fought for independence was to get rid of the European culture. But Chief Nanga raised his children as Mrs Nanga's statement proves: "They would become English people. Don't you see they hardly speak our language?" Ask them something in it and they reply in English. The little one Micah called my mother "a, dirty, bush woman."(34). This is what colonization has wrought upon the culture of the Igbos. Chief Nanga is the Minister of Culture, a man who has no interest in the value of his culture.

Independent Nigeria did not move towards establishing a stable and genuine government and Government policies. Instead, it gave rise to many political parties; each on their side fought towards their own development diverged in their own axis. Lyon's statement of corruption is proved in all three stages in A Man of the People. Due to corrupt politicians like Chief Naga, the economic growth of the country was completely ruined. Chief Nanga and other politicians had lost interest in service towards the nation and they looted the government treasury. Finally, due to the corrupt politicians, the country is demoralized and people have lost confidence. The complete devastation occurred due to their disability of not recognizing who they are and what they are doing? They got freedom from the colonizers and become slaves of their own people.

And then the filth began to flow. The Daily Matchet for instance carried the story which showed that Chief Nanga, who had himself held the portfolio of Foreign Trade until two years ago, had been guilty of the same practice and had built out of the gains three blocks of seventy storey luxury flats at three hundred thousand pounds each in the name of his wife and these flats were immediately released by the British Amalgamated at fourteen hundred a month each. (MOP, 91)

Chaos struck every wing of independent Nigeria. Due to corruption, they had nationwide strikes and there was fear of, the government being dismissed. The people raged with anger that "After seven years of lethargy any action seemed welcome and desirable; the country was ripe and impatient to shed violent exercise the lazy folds of flabby skin and fat it had put on in the greedy years of indolence" (92).

In A Man of the People, Achebe defined many ideals of the individual that led to the devastation of his country. Colonization did bring a changeover, but the real devastation was due to the individual of the society who was overwhelmed with the change and felt they had been incarnated from the traditional Igbo to the so-called civilized man. A traditional Igbo did not even know the words corruption and bribery. His characteristics were hard work and confidence, and these two traditional qualities were completely sacked from them. They became jealous, selfish and self-centred.

Chief Nanga was no longer the Man of the people. He was towards swindling and corrupting his own people. Even Max who inspired Odili in his revolutionary behaviour said "Ours is ours, mine is mine" (115). It is a sarcastic way to put forward the idea that corruption has to have its limits. No one is concerned about the welfare of the country and its development among the countries of the world. Odili is shocked to hear that Max had borrowed ten thousand pounds from Chief Koko to step down from POP. Odili's vision of fighting a clean duel is interrupted by Max receiving money from the opposition party. Corruption was in the air. Death after death occurred, and Max was killed just as it was prophesied by Odili. "If our people understand nothing else they know that a man who takes money from another in return for service must render that service or remain vulnerable to that man's revenge. Neither God nor juju would save him" (117).

Max, though he stepped down from the POP election, could not tolerate the illegal activities imposed by Chief Koko's wife in the election. Max was run over by a jeep of Koko's party members. Immediately, Eunice took a gun and shot Chief Koko to death. The nation was filled with death, riots and conspiracy everywhere. Chief Nanga was elected again but sill the government had fallen. "The people themselves as we have seen had become even more cynical than their leaders and were apathetic into the bargain. 'Let them eat,' was the people's opinion. After all the white men used to do all the eating. Did we commit suicide? 'Of course not. And where is the all-powerful white man today? He came, he ate and he went. But we are still around" (133). Odili decides to pay the bride price from the POP fund. He thinks when so much havoc has taken place there is nothing wrong in doing that. Due to an unstable and chaotic situation, the government was dismissed and "the military had just abolished all the political parties in the country and announced they would remain abolished until the situation became stabilized once again" (136). Vempala insists that if the ancestors of the Igbo society and several other indigenous groups built a culture, which has kept up its basic pattern with an amazing tenacity in spite of the disastrous colonial rule, the least the African nationals of the present could do is to make a sincere and constructive effort to keep it alive and thriving. (132)

The primary sources of conflict in Africa are those that link the internally focused challenges of state-building with those challenges located in externally focused processes both at the regional and global levels. The intermeshing of domestic insecurities and interstate antagonisms creates an autonomous dynamic of regional conflict and therefore the potential for regional actions to either increase or reduce security and cooperation, and thereby to either facilitate or inhibit the construction of more legitimate and affective states (Spector, 86).

"There religion has something childlike about it. They sense a higher being, but they do not keep a firm hold on it; it passes only fleetingly through their heads. This higher being they transfer to the first stone they come across, thus making it their fetish and they discard this fetish if it fails to help them" (Blake 60). "Entirely good-natured and harmless when in a state of calm, they can become suddenly agitated and then commit the most frightful cruelties . . . they do not show an inner impulsc towards culture. In their native country, the most striking despotism prevails" (60).

The encounter between cultures is precisely the moment at which the articulation of signs becomes apparent, caught between the ambivalence, the 'in-between space', of contesting projections and linguistic negotiation. Cultural representation relies, inevitably, on this conjunction, this clash of signification on the borders and limits of cultures, which acknowledge and mediate cultural meaning always as the articulation of difference and otherness (Kanneh 17).

"The social malaise in Nigerian society was political corruption, and what really happened was that there was a tussle for power; the structure of the country was such 186 that there was an inbuilt power struggle, and those who were in power wanted to stay in power. The easiest and simplest way to retain this power, even in a limited area, was to appeal to tribal sentiments, and this was exploited extensively in the '50s and '60s. (Achebe 32, A Talk on Transition) "Colonial violence is a system which constitutes the features of daily life. It is an imposition, an artifice imposed upon local society and is underwritten by the proximity and the readiness of the occupying army" (Giovanucci, 42).

"The outcry against the impact of Western civilization is both serious and loud. Its decadence, oppression and manipulation are decried, and its ambassadors derided. Western missionaries, traders and commissioners preach a gospel that is inhuman. They cheat. But what is perplexing, the critics find, is that the Africans allow themselves to be treated as inferior" (Granquist, 398)Erritouni identifies that In *Anthills of Savannah* Achebe deterritorializes the nation-state, by exposing its failures to connect with the masses, so as to open up a range of possibilities and new horizons that may serve as an antidote to its ills. The nation-state corresponds to what William calls "the dominant". (54)

In a 1987 interview with Anne Rutherford, Achebe rehearses these alternatives, revealing in the process the contradictions they sustain. He asserts that the way out of the morass of the Nigerian nation-state lies in "the few thinking leaders", "elite", "a handful of people" (2-3). "[T]o correct the situation" (2), the elite must "create the circumstances in which the people begin to act with awareness" (3) and must use their 187 special "training and education and qualifications . . . to initiate the upward movement of the people" (5). According to this view, the people lack initiative, insight and the ability to think of alternatives, as they do not naturally belong to "the few thinking" (Erritouni, 51).

The second case pertains to Simon Gikandi's "Chinua Achebe and the Invention of African Literature" (1996). In this essay, Gikandi describes Chinua Achebe's *Things Fall Apart* as a novel that explores "the crisis of culture generated by the collapse of colonial rule." By this, he means that the events chronicled in the novel unfold at precisely that conjectural moment when colonial intervention puts the very survival of Umuofia (Igbo) culture at risk. Elaborating, he refers to Achebe's concern over the psychological "hold" of colonialism over African people and "the traumatic effects of our first confrontation with Europe." In a poignant phrase, he describes the trauma as having activated "the crisis of the soul" (Esonwanne 141).

“Stupid cleverness, barren smartness that defeats ordinary, solid, sensible, people.” (AS26) Those who mismanage affairs would silence criticism by pretending they have facts not available to the rest of us. “And I know it is fatal to engage them on their own ground. Our best weapon against them is to marshal facts, of which they are truly managers, but Passion is our hope and strength, a very present help in trouble" (35).

Anthills of the Savannah is the continuation of where A *Man of the People* was ended. A military regime was established in A Man of the People, which overthrew the corrupt civilian government. Sam Osodi was appointed the President of state and his friend Ikem became the editor of the National Gazette and Chris the Commissioner of Information. Achebe's main idea in the novel is to bring out the defects and effects of the colonial rule that has endangered the society of the military regime. Achebe throws light on the drastic metamorphosis of the civilization from the Igbo traditional society of a man, to the man who holds a President of the state honour.

Achebe's transition in the novel serves as a result of all five novels. Ikem is simultaneously a mbari artist exhibiting Oka Okwu and a modern social critic who by no means denies the unquestionably damaging influence of colonization but urges his nationals to look for immediate causes of their problems. The mixture of traditional and modern in his speech is symbolic of the mixed heritage of today's Nigerians. To communicate his acknowledgement and acceptance of such heritage, Achebe uses his alter-ego Ikem as a peace-maker between tradition and modernity – he blends ancient views on the role of the artist with modern modes of expression and traditional Igbo verbal craftsmanship with the foreign medium such as the English language. (Nemanja, 32)

Anthills of the Savannah "draws direct experience of Achebe as a politician and as an observer of the Nigerian political scene, particularly the military dictatorship of General Ibrahim Babangida" (Pandurang, 149). "Achebe tried to speculate why Nigeria, in many ways so lively and exciting, was so intrinsically ungovernable, seeming to relish, or at least tolerate, chaos above order" (Povey, 22). "Achebe is himself the chief of his village, Ogidi, and at one time he supported Biafran independence from Nigeria. The founder of a journal dedicated to Igbo culture, he is so identified with "Igboness" that his style has been called an Igbo style in contrast to the Yoruba style of Wole Soyinka" (Kortenaar, 59).

"Achebe's invention of the nation requires that he close two circles: the circle joining the national elite and the masses, and another that joins the traditional participatory community of Abazon with the mass society of Kangan" (65). The cruel absurdity of life in Kangan under Sam's rule could conceivably engender ethnic rivalries such as those that have, in the past, torn Nigeria apart. By transforming everyone within the nation-state into an Igbo, Achebe eliminates the disruptive potential of ethnic loyalties. (69)

"In *Anthills of the Savannah*, Achebe longs for consent and descent to reinforce and legitimize each other, as they do in the identities of European nations, where being a native and being a citizen are often conflated. Nations everywhere are artificial, but in Europe, the tropes of consent and descent have been naturalized; in Africa, their artificiality cannot be disguised" (Kortenaar, 70). "*Anthills of the Savannah* shows all aspects of the colonial process from the beginning to end of the colonial contact. It tells the story of three schoolmates, Ikem, Chris and Sam, who became figures in the new regime of the fictional West African Land of Kangan" (Pandey, 74)

"The novel brings forth the aspirations of the educated youth who wish to see rapid changes in their society. They do realize later that it is their own culture and tradition which can lead to reforms and form a new social order"

(Pandey, 75). Pandey quotes The Weekly Star of 15 May 1983has this on the front page under the title 'The Nigerian and Corruption': "Keeping an average Nigerian from being corrupt is like keeping a goat from eating yam". "Achebe reflects the customs and traditions which bound the Igbo people together in the pre-colonial Igbo society. But with the changing course of time, their faith could not remain intact" (91).

"The aftermaths of the Western takeover of the traditional African societies have had different effects on different individuals. Against a background of corruption and erosion of traditional values, the likes of Nanga live solely for themselves amassing wealth by plundering the nation" (Vempala, 114). The society of Kangan had such dark forces which would hinder the peace and development of the people. As Ikem puts it as "the sneaky wolf of a priest in the sheep clothing" (AS, 37) Ikem was not very much worried about authority because the people were ignorant and it was that mass of the people who "laughed at their own humiliation and murder" (37).

The Kanga republic welcomed the change of the military regime because of the leaders who "openly looted our treasury, whose effrontery soiled our national soul" (AS, 39). Odili in *Man of the People* stated that though at present we welcome the change presuming that the military rule would not have an opposition party, he insisted that the military coup will be followed by a counter military coup. After getting rid of corrupt politicians like Chief Nanga the country got into the hard clutches of dictator Sam His Excellency President of the state. As Ikem puts it "Worshipping a dictator was such a pain in the ass" (AS, 41).

Colonization paid a heavy cost for the upbringing of the African savages. The humorous part is that in the course of abusing the white man and his ways, people have totally forgotten that they had black sheep among themselves like Sam. The treasury and the culture of the Igbo tradition, we say had been looted by the white government; then what do we see say, of the contemporary lootings. Cultural conflicts brought such havoc in the society that the people were confused about the disintegrated society. They felt insecure in their own nation. The villain now was not the foreigner, it was his own blood and heir who stood in front of him as a dictator. Chris and Ikem wanted to do service for the country. They thought that Sam would oblige to them but in vain.

Educated people in the Kangan society were mere perverts. Dr Oke is a man who would not move medicine without money. In one of the emergency cases, he demanded money and only then decided to proceed with his treatment. The natives not only suffered at the hands of the Colonizers, but their devastation reached the pinnacle of suffering only in the hands of their own people. Education was to mould an individual for his service towards the society and his country, whereas in the Kangan society it was used to dominate, corrupt and demolish, the ignorance of the people.

Colonization had destroyed all the values in a man. Polygamy was appreciated in the Igbo tradition, but even Monogamy did not thrive in contemporary society. The Africans married European women and they were striving hard to maintain balance in their daily life. But due to the variations in their culture, they did not lead a happy life and some marriages broke as soon as they began. Western culture eroded cultural values.

In spite of revolutionary behaviour, Ikem had a relationship with Elewa and she became pregnant. The youngster of the contemporary Kangan society behaved like an Englishmen and spoke like an African. Achebe has experienced the life of a politician. His observation can be perceived in Anthills of the Savannah: "Public Affairs! They are nothing but the closed transactions of the soldier-turned-politicians, with their cohorts in business and bureaucracy" (135). One of the highlights of devastation is the so-called blood sport known as a public execution. People were killed in the public and there were many who witnessed it without even questioning the height of brutality.

After the military regime took over the fictional nation of the Kangan Republic, youngsters like Chris and Ikem expected a wide exodus in the country. The exodus did happen, but instead of the country Sam the Excellency had a lot of transition in his character. Moreover, he imposed violent dominance, and people were sacked for not obeying him. A vivid example was the death of Ikem Osodi. The prime failure of the government is that the ruler failed to re-establish vital inner links with the poor and dispossessed of this country with the bruised heart that throbs painfully at the core of the nation's being. (AS, 135) "In view of his humble background, Chris believes Okong might serve as a liaison between a government made up mostly of members of the elite and the people. But Okong proves to be an arriviste with no scruples and no self-esteem. His overriding concern to curry favour with the General" (Erritouni, 57)"Experience and intelligence warn us that man's progress in freedom will be piecemeal, slow and unromantic. Revolution may be necessary for taking a society out of an intractable stretch of quagmire but it does not confer freedom and maybe hinder indeed" (AS, 94)

According to Ikem reform is a dirty word. Initially, it gives a lot of hope towards success, but later on, it seems rather impossible. Ikem is in a hardcore relationship with the Excellency and he does not want to hand over the country to a democratic dictatorship. Democracy was proved false, in the rule of the soldier–turned–politician and dictator Sam. Any decision of the country was by Sam, for Sam and of Sam. It was quite disgusting that the Nigerian people had not the courage to rise against the so-called democratic dictatorship.

Achebe throws light on the lack of even the basic needs of society. The country under the rule of Sam the Excellency was devoid of even the basic necessities of life. In a conversation between Chris and the waitress, Achebe guides us to understand the pathetic condition of the people. The women said that she paid one manilla for water and if the scarcity increased they had to pay two manillas. The agitators from Abazon visited Sam to explain about the drought and the difficulties of their living. But he who usurped to do some good for the people denied to meet them. His Excellency was very much considered about securing his positions rather than about the welfare of the nation. "It is the story that outlives the sound of the war drums and the exploit of the brave fighters. ...It is the story that direct us. It is the thing that makes us different from cattle. It is the mark on the face that sets apart from their neighbours" (AS, 119).

Achebe defined Africa as the land of the oppressor than the land of the oppressed. The land was only occupied by a corrupt politicians and government officers who beamed fat with bribery. Bribe hit all the areas of the country. The government workers decided on their own and billing procedures were quite "chaotic billing which was done to cover the massive fraud" (152). "Tribalism, Religious extremism and Electoral Merchandising were the three disasters that hit the nation of Kangan. There was corruption everywhere, and there was no use of a revolution because at the end of the day even the revolutionist had no idea of their protest. Ikem was a straightforward revolutionist who tried to save the country from the dangers of cultural and national exploitation, but he became a victim of his own revolution. He in his lecture at the University of Bassa tried to ignite the students to fight for their rights and work towards the betterment of the country. "In the voices of all of the main characters in the novel, one can clearly recognize Achebe's life experiences, political convictions and sensitivity to struggles that common man in modern African society has to deal with. The long-awaited novel serves as a testimony to the development of the African writer's political ideology and his lifelong commitment to African people" (Mitrovic, 7).

Achebe's main concern was to educate society and liberate them from their blindfolds. Their notion of liberation and freedom from the colonizers was proven false, for their own people behaved worse than the colonizers. As Ikem said people needed a self-examination in order to get rid of this sabotage. 195 Achebe shows the transition of his Igbo civilization in various fragments in his novels. In *Things Fall Apart* the devastation is due to the colonial encounter wherein the basic ideals of a country was slightly disturbed initially and later on due to the havoc it created in the society. It led to the death of a patriot like Okonkwo. In *Arrow of God* Achebe identified the very essence of dilemma among the people as well as the fetish priest Ezeulu. Achebe has shown in this novel the complete takeover of the Christian church and its missionaries due to the idiotic stubbornness of the priest. In *No Longer at Ease*, the beginning of corruption and bribery is very well examined and the reason behind that. Achebe explores the will of his people. It was their acceptance of the change that brought drastic changes in the moral values of the people.A *Man of the People* is the output of the devastation of the society in the hands of the corrupt politicians who have forgotten their Igbo identities and have completely camouflaged with the colonizers' identity. Finally, *Anthills of Savannah* illustrates all the possible contradictions that society would undergo under the military dictatorship. It was very much evident in all the novels that the transition was due to the transformation that occurred in the individual that brought disintegration to the society

9 798885 467650

Printed by Libri Plureos GmbH in Hamburg, Germany